Anonymous

List of Protected Monuments in the United Provinces of Agra

and Oudh

Anonymous

List of Protected Monuments in the United Provinces of Agra and Oudh

ISBN/EAN: 9783337384883

Printed in Europe, USA, Canada, Australia, Japan

Cover: Foto ©ninafisch / pixelio.de

More available books at **www.hansebooks.com**

List of Ancient Protected Monuments

in the

UNITED PROVINCES OF AGRA AND OUDH
(Hindu and Buddhist Monuments)

Serial No.	District.	Locality.	Name of monument.
1	2	3	4
1	Agra	Rajwara, tehsil Agra..	Jaswant Singh-ki-Chhatri
2	Do.	Khairgarh tehsil, 18 miles S.-W. of Agra.	Old tila about 400' to the north of the village and another mound called Tasu Tila about 500' to the east in which ancient sculptures are often found.
3	Do.	Jagner, tehsil Khairgarh	Gawal Baba temple with the stairway leading thereto and the Baoli outside, below the main gateway of the fort.
4	Aligarh	Gorsedhana, tehsil Iglas	Three mounds
5	Do.	Rajira Khera, about 4 miles to the west of Akarabad on the south side of the Koal road about 1½ miles to the west of the great Bridge over the Ganges Canal.	Khera mound measuring 760' from north to south by 80' from east to west, greatest elevation being about 35'.
6	Do.	Do.	A smaller mound measuring 112' × 107' ..
7	Do.	Sahegarh Khera, 6 miles to the N.-E. of Akarabad.	Sahegarh Khera, a very deserted and extensive mound situated about 1,300' to the S.-E. of the small Garhi or mud fort and about 2,120' to the S.-E. of Sahegarh village. The mound measures 100' × 530', the greatest height being 60'.
8	Do.	Do.	Nagaria Khera about a mile to the west of Sahegarh Khera.
9	Do.	Sankra in tehsil Atrauli, 36 miles E. of Aligarh.	An extensive ancient site which consists of the remains of an ancient fort and of an extensi Khera.
10	Do.	Do.	Mound about 700' long, 300' to the east of Sankar part of which appears to be the remains of Buddhist Stupa or of a temple.
11	Do.	Do.	One high isolated conical-shaped mound
12	Do.	Sasani in tehsil Hathras, 14 miles south of Aligarh.	A large and conspicuous mound called Gohar Khera, an old Buddhist establishment, at a sho distance from the town.
13	Allahabad	Allahabad, tehsil Allahad.	Asoka stone pillar in the fort ..
14	Do.	Bhita	Ancient monuments
15	Do.	Sheorajpur	Garhwa Fort

Owner or owners	Whether in use for religious purposes.	Whether an agreement exists.	Number and date of Notification confirming protection.	Remarks.	Serial No.
5	6	7	8	9	10
Private	Yes	No	758-M., dated 31st March 1910.		1
Do.	Yes	No	1669-M./1133-M., dated 27th Dec. 1920.		2
Nazul land	Yes		1299-M./357, dated 21st Oct. 1916.		3
Private	No	No	1475-M./367-9. dated 24th June 1913.		4
Do.	No	No	1669-M./1133-M., dated 27th Dec. 1920.		5
Do.	No	No	Do.		6
Do.	No	No	Do.		7
			Do.		8
Government and private.	No	No	Do.		9
Private	No	No	Do.		10
Do.	No	No	Do.		11
Do.	No	No	Do.		12
Government	No		1645-1133, dated 22nd Dec. 1920.		13
...ate	No	Yes	1881-M./357, dated 3rd Nov. 1910.		14
	Yes	Yes	911-M./367-4, dated 27th June 1911.		15

Serial No.	District.	Locality.	Name of monument.
1	2	3	4
16	Allahabad	Karra ..	The fort which is attributed to Jayachandra, the last Hindu Raja of Kanauj.
17	Do. ..	Kosam (Ancient Kausambi).	The ancient fortress (representing the ancient Kausambi) which has a circuit of about 4 miles.
18	Do.	Pabhosa, a small village on the north bank of Jumna in tehsil Manjhanpur, 32 miles S.-W. of Allahabad.	Artificial cave in the face of the hill of Pabhosa, 3 miles to the N.-W. of the fort of Kosam.
19	Do.	Do. ..	Traces of a large brick building on the summit of the Pabhosa hill 200′ above the cave.
20	Do.	Singraur, village in tehsil Sarson, 18 miles N.-W. of Allahabad.	A large mound 18′ high, 50′ broad at top and 150′ at base strewn with brickbats and called Surya Bhita.
21	Do. .. .	Dalelganj, Allahabad	Statue of a horse sculptured in white sand-stone which was exhumed from a field near the village of Dalelganj ½ mile to the west of the fort.
22	Do.	Mankuar	Cave known as Sita-ki-Rasoi containing an inscription in three lines of well formed characters of the 9th century A. D.
23	Do.	Sarpur, ⅓ a mile to the N.-E. of Bikar and beyond the end of the hills.	A small square obelisk or lower part of a pillar with a Gupta inscription of 13 lines on one face containing the name of Kumaragupta Mahendra.
24	Do.	Chilla, small village in tehsil Bara, 14 miles S.-W. of Allahabad.	Large stone dwelling house said to have been the residence of the two heroes Ala and Udal, Cir. 8th century A. D.
25	Do.	The Ganja Hill, an isolated mountain in tehsil Bara, 40 miles S.-W. of Allahabad close to the exit of the Tons river from the Vindhya hills.	A rocky hall bearing an inscription of three lines of the Indo-Scythian period in red paint with some rude drawings of men and animals.
26	Do.	Jhusi ..	Ruined forts of Samudragupta and Hamsagupta which have yielded gold coins of Kumaragupta.
27	Almora	Jageswar	Temple of Jageswar .. .. ..
28	Do. ..	Do	Temple of Mrityunjaya .. .. ..
29	Do.	Do.	Navadevi or Nau Durga Shrine ..

Owner or owners.	Whether in use for religious purposes.	Whether an agreement exists.	Number and date of Notification confirming protection.	Remarks.	Serial No.
5	6	7	8	9	10
Government	No	..	1669-M./1133-M., dated 27th Dec. 1920.		16
Private ..	Yes ..	No ..	Do.		17
Do. ..	Yes ..	No ..	Do.		18
Do. ..	Yes ..	No ..	Do.		19
Do. ..	Yes ..	No ..	Do.		20
Government	No ..		Do.		21
Private	No ..	No ..	Do.		22
..		..	Do.		23
Government	No ..		Do.		24
Private ..	Yes ..	No ..	Do.		25
Do. ..	Yes ..	No ..	Do.		26
Public ..	Yes ..	Yes ..	896-M./367-38, dated 20th/29th May 1915.		27
Do. ..	Yes ..	Yes ..	Do.		28
Do. ..	Yes ..	Yes ..	Do.		29

Serial No.	District.			Locality.			Name of monument.
1	2			3			4
30	Almora	..	..	Jageswar	..	..	Surya shrine .. ..
31	Do.		..	Do.		..	Navagraha shrine ..
32	Do.	..	..	Do.		..	Pyramidal shrine .. ..
33	Do.		..	Do.		..	Kuvera shrine ..
34	Do.	..	..	Do.		..	Temple of Chandika Devi ..
35	Do.	..	..	Do.		..	Dandeswar temple .. ..
36	Do.	..	..	Dwarahat	..	..	Group of temples, a site known locally as Kacheri
37	Do.		..	Do.		..	Gujardeo temple, close to the Syalde Pokhar ..
38	Do.	..	..	Do.		..	Group of temples, known as Maniyan ..
39	Do.	..	..	Do.	..	..	Group of temples, known as Ratan Deo, west of Gujar Deo temple.
40	Do.	..	..	Do.		..	Badarinath temple .. .. ..
41	Do.		..	Do.	..	..	Mrityunjaya temple .. ..
42	Do.		..	Do.	..	..	Bandeo temple on the left bank of Khiro ..
43	Do.		..	Do.		..	Kutumbari Deo temple .. .. ..
44	Do.	..	..	Champawat		..	Naula ..
45	Do.		..	Do.		..	Kotwali Chabutra .. ..
46	Do.		..	Do.	..	..	Baleswar temple with subsidiary shrines and enclosure wall.
47	Do.		..	Baijnath or Vaidyanath a village in pargana Danpur of Almora tehsil.			A large Hindu temple sacred to Kali in the old Ranchula fort and several other old temples of usual style together with the masonry wall containing two inscriptions of Udayapaladeva.
48	Do.	..	..	Gangoli hat in Champawat tehsil.			Remains of a few old temples and an inscribed masonry well close to the S.-W. of the village.
49	Do.		..	Katarmal, pargana Baramandal, tehsil Almora.			A large temple dedicated to the Sun .. ..
50	Azamgarh	..	..	Pakri, near Dabbaon, 26 miles south of Azamgarh.			Inscribed stone pillar .. ..

AGRA AND OUDH—contd.

MONUMENTS—contd.

Owner or owners.	Whether in use for religious purposes.	Whether an agreement exists.	Number and date of Notification confirming protection.	Remarks.	Serial No.
5	6	7	8	9	10
Public ..	Yes ..	Yes ..	896-M./367-28, dated 20th/ 28th May 1915.		30
Do. ..	Yes ..	Yes ..	Do.		31
Do. ..	Yes ..	Yes ..	Do.		32
Do. ..	Yes ..	Yes ..	Do.		33
Do. ..	Yes ..	Yes ..	Do.		34
Do. ..	Yes ..	Yes ..	Do.		35
Government	Yes .	..	830-M./367-28, dated 10th/ 15th May 1915.		36
Do. ..	Yes		Do.		37
Do. ..	Yes	..	Do.		38
Do. ..	Yes ..	..	Do.		39
Dwarahat people.	Yes ..	Yes ..	Do.		40
Government	Yes ..	..	Do.		41
Do. ..	Yes .	..	Do.		42
Do. ..	Yes ..	..	Do.		43
Do. ..	Yes ..		1233-M./367-36, dated 13th Oct. 1916.		44
Do. ..	Yes ..	..	Do.		45
Private ..	Yes ..	Yes ..	Do.		46
Public ..	Yes ..	..	1069-M./1133-M. dated 27th Dec. 1920.		47
Private ..	Yes ..	No ..	Do.		48
Public ..	Yes ..	No ..	Do.		49
Private ..	Yes ..	No ..	1645-M./1133, dated 22nd Dec. 1920.		50

Serial No.	District.			Locality.	Name of monument.
1	2			3	4
51	Bahraich	..	..	Chandra or Chahardha village in tehsil Nanpura, 26 miles north of Bahraich.	A large brick-strewn khera, being the ruins of an apparently Buddhist city.
52	Do.		..	Tandwa, old village in pargana Ikauna of tehsil Bahraich, 20 miles east of head-quarters.	A mound of brick ruins 800' × 300' ..
53	Banda	..	..	Bhawanipur, 3 miles south of Chilla, tehsil Pailani.	Baoli .. ..
54	Do.		..	Karwi	Temple in the centre of a tank near Jail ..
55	Do.		..	Do. ..	Stone temple in Ganesh Bagh, 1 mile S.-E. of Karwi.
56	Do.	..	..	Ansuyaji, famous pilgrimage place on the south bank of the Paisuni in Karwi, 15 miles south of the tehsil.	Two inscriptions, one dated 1520, the other undated on a large basalt rock close to the bank of the river.
57	Do.	..	..	Gulrampur, tehsil Badausa.	Balaria Math, 2 miles north of Gulrampur ..
58	Do.	..	..	Dadhwamanpur-Gulrampur village in tehsil Badausa, 12 miles south of tehsil.	Remains of an old Chandella temple .. ..
59	Do.		..	Gonda village in tehsil Badausa, 6 miles S.-E. of tehsil and 30 miles S.-E. of Banda.	Two Chandella temples standing together on the same platform.
60	Do.	..	..	Gulrampur village in tehsil Badausa, 16 miles S.-E. of tehsil.	Remains of two temples situated towards the south of the hill near the village.
61	Do.		..	Rasin, tehsil Badausa	Remains of an old fort and disused temple of Devi Chandi Mahesvari on the summit of a hill.
62	Do.		..	Do. ..	Several Sati pillars with a large standing female figure holding a child in her left arm.
63	Do.		..	Do. ..	The famous temple of Chandi Mahesvari in a dense jungle on the top of a hill about 1 mile to the east of the village of Rasin.
64	Do.		..	Do. ..	A rock-hewn tank 80' × 50' close to the temple of Chandi Maheshvari.

Owner or owners.	Whether in use for religious purposes.	Whether an agreement exists.	Number and date of Notification confirming protection.	Remarks.	Serial No.
5	6	7	8	9	10
Balrampur Estate.	No ..	No ..	1669-M./1133-M., dated 27th Dec. 1920.		51
Kapurthala Estate.	Yes ..	No ..	Do.		52
Private ..	No ..	No ..	1645-M./1133, dated 22nd Dec. 1920.		53
Government	No ..	..	Do.		54
Private ..	No ..	No ..	Do.		55
Do. ..	Yes ..	No ..	1669-M./1133-M., dated 27th Dec. 1920.		56
Government	No ..	..	1645-M./1133, dated 22nd Dec. 1920.		57
Do. ..	No ..		1669-M./1133-M., dated 27th Dec. 1920.		58
Do. ..	No ..	..	Do.		59
Do. ..	No ..		Do.		60
Do. ..	No ..		1645-M./1133, dated 22nd Dec. 1920.		61
Do. ..	Yes ..		1669-M./1133-M., dated 27th Dec. 1920.		62
Do. ..	No ..		Do.		63
Do. ..	No ..	..	Do.		64

Serial No.	District.	Locality.	Name of monument.
1	2	3	4
65	Banda	Rasin, tehsil Badausa	Remains of a small Chandella temple near the village of Birpur 2 miles S.-W. of Rasin.
66	Do.	Marpha hill fort in tehsil Badausa, 8 miles south of tehsil.	The great fort of Marpha situated on a high projecting hill 12 miles to the N.-E. of Kalinjar with the fortification walls and the three ruined Jain temples and one ruined Hindu temple inside the fort.
67	Do.	Bahra-Kotra, two small villages on the south bank of the Jumna, in tehsil Mau, 11 miles east of tehsil.	Remains of a temple, Circa 10th Century A. D., usually called Bhar Deul.
68	Do.	Do. ..	Two large caves known by the name of Rikhian in the face of the hill nearly due south from Barha Kotra and about 1½ miles distant.
69	Do.	Do. ..	A small temple with a sanctum only 4'-10" square and a flat roof situated outside the caves.
70	Do.	Do. ..	Two temples in ruins .. ..
71	Do. ..	Lauri or Lokhari village in tehsil Mau, 10 miles N.-E. of tehsil.	Ruins of some Jain temples on the bank of the lake and in the fields.
72	Do. ..	Mau tehsil on the right bank of the Jumna.	Two ruined temples of small size of fine workmanship, 1½ miles to the S.-W. of Mau near the hamlet of Rithara.
73	Do.	Do. ..	Ruins of a large Linga temple of the Chandella type, the sanctum of which is standing 5 miles to the west of Mau in the hamlet of Pura, close to the village of Hatovar.
74	Do.	Do. ..	A two-storeyed priests' house consisting of ten cells, a good specimen of the mediæval Hindu domestic architecture.
75	Do. ..	Ramnagar in tehsil Mau, 10 miles west of tehsil.	The ruins of a large Chandella temple. The sanctum is entirely gone but the mandapa remains.
76	Do.	Do. ..	Remains of a large temple, 1½ miles to the west of Ramnagar on the high road leading to Karwi.
77	Do. ..	Kalinjar, tehsil Naraini	Approaches to Kalinjar Fort .. ..
78	Do.	Do. ..	The fort of Kalinjar together with the parapet walls with the Gateways and the monuments inside it, viz., Sita Kund, Sita Sej, Patalganga, and Pandu Kund and with Bhairon-ka-Jhirka, Sidh-ki-Gupha, Bhagwan Sej, Pani-ka-aman, the Mrigdhara, Kotitirth, the Linga temple of Nilakantha, etc.

AGRA AND OUDH—contd.

MONUMENTS— contd.

Owner or owners.	Whether in use for religious purposes.	Whether an agreement exists.	Number and date of Notification confirming protection.	Remarks.	Serial No.
5	6	7	8	9	10
Government	No	..	1669-M./1133-M., dated 27th Dec. 1920.		65
Do.	Yes	..	Do.		66
Private	No	No	Do.		67
Do.	No	No	Do.		68
Do.	No	No	Do.		69
Do.	No	No	Do.		70
Do.	No	No	Do.		71
Do.	No	No	Do.		72
Do.	No	No	Do.		73
			Do.		74
Private	No	No	Do.		75
Do.	No	No	Do.		76
Government	No	..	1645-M./1133, dated 22nd Dec. 1920.		77
Do.	Yes	..	1669-M./1133-M., dated 27th Dec. 1920.		78

Serial No.	District.		Locality.	Name of monument.
1	2		3	4
79	Banda	.. ..	Khoh, 1 mile distant from the village of Kalu.	Ruins of an old temple, called Haihait Mandir on the top of a picturesque hill, together with fragments of statues scattered about the foot of the hill.
80	Bareilly	.. ..	Ramnagar	Mounds to the south of the tanks known as the Gandhan Sagar and the Adi Sagar.
81	Do.	..	Do. ..	A small hillock called Katari Khera or Kottari Khera where Cunningham unearthed the plinth of a small temple and Jain figures and railing pillars.
82	Do.	..	Do. ..	Mound called Chikatia Khera at a short distance to the S.-W. of Kotari Khera, apparently the site of a Buddhist Vihara.
83	Do.	.. ..	Do.	Two Buddhist mounds on the N.-W. corner of the great bastion close to the Konwaru Tal.
84	Do.	.. ..	Do. ..	Fort at Ramnagar or Ahichhatra, ancient, capital of northern Panchala. It is over 3½ miles in circumference and its interior is covered with old brick foundations. The highest mound on the site is 68' above the level of the ground.
85	Do.	.. ..	Do. ..	Stupa mound standing on a great irregular mound nearly a mile due west of the N.-W. corner of the Ramnagar fortress and about the same distance N.-N.-E. of Ramnagar. The ruin is 30' in diameter and 40' in height.
86	Do.	..	Pachaumi or Vahidpur Pachaumi (the ancient Pancha-bhumi) in tehsil Faridpur, 16 miles S.-E. of Bareilly.	Several ancient ruined mounds in which Indo-Scythian coins are found.
87	Basti	.. ..	Maghar	The double shrine of Kabir Shah (Hindu portion)
88	Do.	.. ..	Piprahva, Birdpur Estate, pargana Bansi East.	The site of the stupa and monastery of the Sakyas
89	Do.	..	Pipri	Ancient site ..
90	Banaras	.. ..	Sarnath'	All the ancient monuments on the Buddhist site ..
91	Do.	.. ..	Do. ..	The whole of the area to the east of the Buddhist site explored by the Archæological Department extending up to the limits of the lake named Narokhar. Also the area around Archæological site at Sarnath on which erection of buildings, etc., is restricted subject to approval as to design and material, by the Archæological Department.

GRA AND OUDH—contd.

[ONUMENTS—contd.

Owner or owners.	Whether in use for religious purposes.	Whether an agreement exists.	Number and date of Notification confirming protection.	Remarks.
5	6	7	8	9
Private ..	Yes ..	No ..	1669-M./113-M., dated 27th Dec. 1920.	
Do. ..	No ..	No ..	Do.	
Do. ..	No ..	No ..	Do.	
Do. ..	No ..	No ..	Do.	
Do. ..	No ..	No ..	Do.	
Do. ..	No ..	No ..	Do. ..	The small temple inside the fort is in use for religious purposes.
Do. ..	No ..	No ..	Do.	
Do. ..	No ..	No ..	Do.	
Do. ..	Yes ..	No ..	619-M./367-52, dated 22nd May 1917.	
Do. ..	No ..	No ..	706-M.S./110-M.S.—1927, dated 27th August 1928.	
Do. ..	No ..	No ..		
Government	No ..		..	
Government and private.	No ..		1669-M./1133-M., 706-M.S./110-M.S.—1927, dated 27th August 1928.	

Serial No.	District.		Locality.	Name of monument.
1	2		3	4
92	Benares ..	..	Benares City ..	The Observatory of Man Singh .. ..
93	Do.	..	Do. ..	The Pahladpur inscribed lat or monolith now standing in the compound of the Queen's College at Benares.
94	Do.	..	Do. ..	Georgian Grave near Isvar Gangi Siva temple ..
95	Do.	..	Bakariya Kund in the Jaitpur division of Benares City.	Buddhist temple ..
96	Do.	..	Chandrauti (Chandravati), old village in pargana Katihar, 14 miles N.-E. from Benares.	Remains of a massive brick fort on the left bank of the Ganges.
97	Do.	..	Bairant, a village in pargana Bara of tehsil Chandauli, 16 miles S.-E. of Benares.	A very extensive ancient site on the south bank of the Ramganga. It measures about 1,350' long and 900' broad and consists of a very ancient ruined fort.
98	Do.	..	Tilmapur	An ancient mound .. ..
99	Do.	..	Zamania, pargana Mahaich.	An old ruined Kot (fortress) at a distance of 14 miles west of Zamania.
100	Do.	..	Dhanpur village in pargana Mahaich of tehsil Zamania, 16 miles S.-W. of Ghazipur.	A large mound of brick ruins about half a mile to the north of the village.
101	Bijnore	..	Tehsil Najibabad ..	Mordhaj, also known as Munawar Jar with lofty mound situated 27 miles N.-E. of Bijnore near the railway line of Kotdwar.
102	Do. ..	..	Tip, small village in pargana Mandawar of tehsil Bijnore on the left bank of the Ganges Khadir, 15 miles N.-N.-E. of headquarters.	A mound of great age which was excavated in 1886 and yielded five gold coins of the Kushan king Vasudeva.
103	Bulandshahr	..	Dankaur, tehsil Sikandarabad.	Masonry tank and ancient temple ..
104	Do.	..	Aurangabad Chandhok, an old village in pargana Bhikapur.	Ruins of an old temple known as Chandrani-ka-mandir.
105	Do. ..	..	Bulandshahr ..	A large mound to the west of modern town. The mound is popularly known under the name of Moti Bazaar.

Owner or owners.	Whether in use for religious purposes.	Whether an agreement exists.	Number and date of Notification confirming protection.	Remarks.	Serial No.
5	6	7	8	9	10
Jaipur State	No ..	No ..	1669-M./1133-M., dated 27th Dec. 1920.		92
Government	No	..	Do.		93
Private ..	Yes ..	No ..	5099-M./27-1926, dated 9th Dec. 1926.		94
			1645-M./1133, dated 22nd Dec. 1920.		95
Do. ..	Yes ..	No ..	1669-M./1133-M., dated 27th Dec. 1920.		96
Do. ..	No ..	No	Do.	There is a small platform dedicated to goddess Devi which is used for religious purposes.	97
Do. ..	No ..	Yes ..	5014-M./51, dated 2nd Dec. 1926.		98
Do. ..	No ..	No ..	1645-M./1133 dated 22nd Dec. 1920.		99
Do. ..	No ..	No ..	1669-M./1133-M., dated 27th Dec. 1920.		100
Do. ..	No ..	No ..	1645-M./1133, dated 22nd Dec. 1920.		101
Do. ..	No ..	No ..	1669-M./1133-M., dated 27th Dec. 1920.		102
Do. ..	Yes ..	No ..	1645-M./1133, dated 22nd Dec. 1920.		103
Do. ..	Yes ..	No ..	1669-M./1133-M., dated 27th Dec. 1920.		104
Do. ..	No ..	No ..	Do.		105

Serial No.	District.			Locality.		Name of monument.
1	2			3		4
106	Bulandshahr	..		Bulandshahr	..	Balai Kot or upper fort at Bulandshahr which is pointed out as the remains of buildings erected by Haradatta who ruled at the time of Mahmud of Ghazni's invasion.
107	Do.	..	..	Indore on the right bank of the eastern branch of the Choya Nadi, ¼ mile to the W.-N.-W. of Anupshahr-Koel road and about 8 miles S.-S.-W. of Anupshahr.		A very large and lofty mound with a small village perched on the E.-N.-E. side of it.
108	Do.	..	..	Do.	..	Kundanpur mound or the great temple mound ..
109	Do.		..	Do.	..	Ahirpur mound or lesser temple mound situated about 225' to the south of the Kundanpura mound. This mound measures about 125' × 110'.
110	Do.	..	..	Do.	..	Vaidyapura mounds including four mounds situated to the north side of the Indore Khera across the Choya Nadi.
111	Do.	..	..	Ahar	..	Several large tumuli (kheras) in and about Ahar ..
112	Cawnpur	..	..	Bhitargaon or Bahari Bhitari village in tehsil Narwal, 20 miles south of Cawnpur.		A mound of ruins covered with large bricks and broken figures at a distance of 580' nearly due south of the Bhitargaon temple.
113	Do.	..	..	Do.	..	The site of ancient brick temple together with the whole area of land within the compound wall.
114	Do.	..	..	Parauli, tehsil Narwal		The site of temple known as Mahadeo Baba together with a strip of land 3 yards around it.
115	Do.	..	..	Bihpur near Rar, tehsil Ghatampur.		The site of temple known as " Phulmati Devi " together with a strip of land 2 yards wide on 3 sides of the temple site.
116	Do.		..	Simbhua, tehsil Cawnpur.		The site of temple together with a strip of land 3 yards wide around its plinth.
117	Do.		..	Bithur, tehsil Cawnpur		The remains of the fort of Uttanapada ..
118	Do.		..	Beda-Bedauna	..	Ancient brick temple covered with whitewashed and carved bricks, mouldings, etc.
119	Do.		..	Khurda	..	Two ancient brick temples decorated with panels which are filled with terracotta images.
120	Do.		..	Kanchilpur	..	One ancient brick temple built on the same plan as Bhitargaon temple.

AGRA AND OUDH—*contd.*

MONUMENTS—*contd.*

Owner or owners.	Whether in use for religious purposes.	Whether an agreement exists.	Number and date of Notification confirming protection.	Remarks.	Serial No.
5	6	7	8	9	10
Nazul	No	..	1669-M./1133-M., dated 27th Dec. 1920.		106
Private	No	No	Do.		107
Do.	No	No	Do.		108
Do.	No	No	Do.		109
Do.	No	No	Do.		110
Do.	No	No	Do.		111
Government	Yes	..	Do.		112
Do.	No		1317-M./367, dated 15th May 1909.		113
Do.	No		Do.		114
Do.	Yes		Do.		115
Do.	Yes		Do.		116
Do.	Yes		213-M./357, dated 1st Feb. 1912.		117
Private	Yes	No	1669-M./1133-M., dated 27th Dec. 1920.		118
Do.	No	No	Do.		119
Government	Yes		Do.		120

Serial No.	District.			Locality.		Name of monument.
1	2			3		4
121	Cawnpur	..	..	Sarhar-Amauli	..	Two brick temples built on the same plan and in the same style of ornament and architecture as those at Rar.
122	Do.	..	..	Subhanpur	..	A long Sanskrit inscription in the well of Gayadin Sukal.
123	Do.	..	..	Behta, a small village, 2 miles to the south of Bhitargaon.		Three images of Lakshmana, Ganesa and Vishnu lying in the cells on each side of the doorway of the temple of Jagan Nath, a Gupta pillar lying in the compound of the temple and other images lying in a neglected condition.
124	Dehra Dun		..	Kalsi	.. ..	The inscribed rock edicts of Asoka .. ..
125	Do.	..	..	Lakha Mandal, 24 miles from Chakrata.		Temple and images in its vicinity .. ..
126	Do.	..	..	Bankauli near Madha		An old temple of Mahasu or Mahadeva. The shrine is built on a Tibetan model.
127	Do.	..	..	Hanol or Onol about 15 miles N.-E. of Madha.		Famous temple sacred to Mahasu ..
128	Do.	..	..	Rikhi Kesh on the Ganges, 25 miles east of Dehra Dun.		An old Hindu temple said to have been built by Sankaracharya about 674 A. D.
129	Etah	..	..	Sakit	.. ..	Fort .. ..
130	Do.	..	..	Soron, tehsil Kasganj		Sita Ramji's temple .. .. ..
131	Do.		..	Noh Khas, tehsil Jalesar.		Two mounds together with ancient sculptures and other antiquarian remains at Noh Khas and Noh Khera together with ancient sculptures and other antiquarian remains exclusive of the female image locally known as Rukmini Devi.
132	Do.	..	..	Atraunji Khera village in tehsil Etah, 10 miles north of headquarters.		A large mound 3,960′ long, 1,500′ broad, and 65′ high, the site of some ancient and important place.
133	Do.	.	..	Basundra village in tehsil Etah, 10 miles S.-W. of headquarters.		Khera Basundra, one of the old Chauhan strongholds
134	Do.		..	Bilsar	.. ..	The site of Gupta remains .. .. ..
135	Do.		..	Do.	..	Large mound, more than 33′ high standing in the very midst of the village and dividing it into two distinct portions, known as Bilsar Pachhiya and Bilsar Purva.

AGRA AND OUDH—*contd.*

MONUMENTS—*contd.*

Owner or owners.	Whether in use for religious purposes.	Whether an agreement exists.	Number and date of Notification confirming protection.	Remarks.	Serial No,
5	6	7	8	9	10
Government	..		1669-M./1133-M., dated 27th Dec. 1920.		121
Private ..	No ..	No ..	Do.		122
Government	Yes ..		Do.		123
Do. ..	No .		3119-M./367, dated 23rd Nov, 1909.		124
Private ..	Yes ..	No ..	3123-M./367, dated 23rd Nov. 1909.		125
H. H. the Maharaja of Tehri State.			1669-M./1133-M., dated 27th Dec. 1920.		126
Private ..	Yes ..	No ..	Do.		127
Do. ..	Yes ..	No ..	Do.		128
Government	Yes ..		1645-M./1133, dated 22nd Dec. 1920.		129
Do. ..	No ..		Do.		130
Private ..	Yes ..	No ..	1471-M./367-9, dated 24th June 1913.		131
Do. ..	Yes	No	1669-M./1133-M., dated 27th Dec. 1920.		132
Do. ..	No .	No	Do.		133
Government	No ..		706-M.S./110-M.S.—1927, dated 27th August 1928.		134
Do. ..	No ..		1669-M./1133-M.. dated 27th Dec. 1920.		135

Serial No.	District.	Locality.	Name of monument.
1	2	3	4
136	Etah	Malavan village in tehsil Etah, 13 miles S.-E. of headquarters.	Remains of an old temple, the foundation of which was built with large bricks measuring 15″×8″× 2¼″ to 5½″ in thickness.
137	Etawah	Chakarnagar	The ancient mound including the old fortress measuring about 1 square mile.
138	Do.	Asai Khera a small village in tehsil Etawah, 7 miles west of headquarters on the right bank of the Jumna.	Remains of an old fort built by Chandrapala
139	Fatehpur	Tindauli, pargana Bindhki.	The site of a temple together with whole area of land situated within 100 yards of the site.
140	Do	Bahua, pargana Ghazipur.	The site of a temple together with whole area of land situated within 100 yards of the site.
141	Do.	Kurari, 2 miles north of Bahua.	The site of four temples together with whole area of land situated within 100 yards of the site.
142	Do.	Thithura, pargana Fatehpur.	The site of two temples together with whole area of land situated within 100 yards of the site
143	Do.	Saton, 4 miles from Bahrampur, pargana Fatehpur.	The site of a temple together with whole area of land situated within 100 yards of the site.
144	Do.	Aphui village in tehsil Khaga, 29 miles S.-E. of Fatehpur.	A mound 10′ to 12′ in height, covered with broken bricks. It is called Chauki because it was one of the stages on the old Hindu road from Kanauj to Prayag.
145	Do.	Kutila village in tehsil Khaga, 19 miles east of Fatehpur.	Ruins of a fort built by Jaya Chandra on the bank of the Ganges.
146	Do.	Asni village, in tehsil Fatehpur, 10 miles north of headquarters.	A large mound covered with broken bricks and pottery on the very brink of the Ganges on a projecting promontory within the land of Chak-Pihana. The mound is about 900′ square. On the top of the mound is a platform dedicated to Damabir.
147	Do.	Municipal Garden at Fatehpur.	Square sand-stone pillar bearing an inscription of Mahipaladeva, dated S. 974.
148	Do.	Do. do.	A collection of miscellaneous antiquities from different parts of the district grouped around the Asni pillar of Mahipaladeva.

AGRA AND OUDH—*contd.*

MONUMENTS—*contd.*

Owner or owners.	Whether in use for religious purposes.	Whether an agreement exists.	Number and date of Notification confirming protection.	Remarks.	Serial No.
5	6	7	8	9	10
Private	Yes	No	1669-M./1133-M., dated 27th Dec. 1920.		136
Do.	No	No	1861-M./367-20, dated 28th Oct. 1914.		137
Do.	Yes	No	Do.		138
Do.	Yes	No	1317-M./367, dated 15th May 1909.		139
Do.	Yes	No	Do.		140
Do.	Yes	No	Do.		141
Do.	No	No	Do.		142
Do.	No	No	2611-M./367, dated 25th Sep. 1906.		143
Do.	No	No	1669-M./1133-M., dated 27th Dec. 1920.		144
Do.	No	No	Do.		145
Do.	Yes	No	Do.		146
Government	No	..	Do.		147
Do.	No	..	Do.		148

Serial No.	District.		Locality.	Name of monument.
1	2		3	4
149	Fatehpur	..	Asothar village in tehsil Ghazipur, 14 miles S.-E.-S. of Fatehpur.	An extensive brick-strewn mound, 2 or 3 furlongs to the south of the fort built by Araru Singh.
150	Do.	..	Do. do. ..	A smaller mound further to the south of the above, bearing 5 large Digambar Jain figures which people call the five Pandavas.
151	Do.	..	Tiksariya village ..	An extensive mound evidently an ancient site and a group of Hindu sculptures.
152	Do.	.. ..	Paina village about 2 miles to the north of Ghazipur.	Extensive ruins of an ancient fortified town said to be a stronghold of the Chandellas though it may be of still higher antiquity.
153	Do.	..	Hathgaon	A stone elephant called Jagannath lying about 2 miles from Hathgaon near the spot where the Sasur Khaderi river crosses the road to Hussainganj.-
154	Do.	..	Khairai village in tehsil Khakhreru. 25 miles S.-E.-S. of Fatehpur.	A circular mound the site of a temple, of which only the foundations remain in situ with traces of broad flight of steps.
155	Do.	.. ..	Do. do. ..	An extensive mound called Garhi .. ..
156	Garhwal	.. ..	Adbadri village in pargana Chandpur.	Remains of 16 temples ..
157	Do.	.. ..	Chandpur in pargana Chandpur.	The fort with walls and ruins of dwelling houses inside it and with flights of steps.
158	Do.	..	Gopeswar village in pargana Nurpur.	A trident of iron with a shaft 16' high, with one ancient and three modern inscriptions situated in the compound of a fine old temple which was repaired by Amar Sinha Thapa.
159	Do.	..	Barahat ..	A trident of iron with a shaft of the same material with an ancient inscription.
160	Ghazipur	..	.	Bhitari, tehsil Saidpur, 20 miles west of Ghazipur on the left bank of the Gangi Nadi.	Most important remains in the district belonging to the Gupta period and amongst the oldest Brahmanical remains known.
161	Do.	..	Do. do. ..	The Bhitari Gupta pillar with an inscription of Skandagupta standing in the ruined fort.
162	Do.	..	A small village in tehsil Saidpur, 26 miles west of Ghazipur.	An enormous mound known as Masaon-Dih ..
163	Do.	..	Latiya, small village in tehsil Zamaniya, 13½ miles south of Ghazipur.	A stone lat or pillar standing on the western end of a mound of brick ruins about 500' × 200' and the capital of the pillar lying on the ground close by.

MONUMENTS—contd.

Owner or owners.	Whether in use for religious purposes.	Whether an agreement exists.	Number and date of Notification confirming protection.	Remarks.	Serial No.
5	6	7	8	9	10
Private ..	Yes ..	No ..	1669-M./1133-M., dated 27th Dec. 1920.		149
Do. ..	Yes ..	No ..	Do.		150
Do. ..	Yes ..	No ..	Do.		151
Do. ..	No ..	Yes ..	Do.		152
Do. ..	Yes ..	No ..	Do.		153
Do. ..	No ..	No ..	Do.		154
Do. ..	No ..	No ..	Do.		155
Public ..	Yes ..	No ..	Do.		156
Government ..	No ..		Do.		157
Public ..	Yes ..	No ..	Do.		158
Tehri State ..			Do.		159
Government ..	No ..		1645-M./1133, dated 22nd Dec. 1920.		160
Do. ..	No ..		1669-M./1133-M., dated 27th Dec. 1920.		161
Private ..	No ..	No ..	Do.		162
Do. ..	No ..	No ..	Do.		163

Serial No.	District.	Locality.	Name of monument.
1	2	3	4
164	Ghazipur	Saidpur tehsil, 24 miles west of Ghazipur.	Two statues representing Varaha or the Boar incarnation and Krishna with Gopis.
165	Do.	Shaikhanpur, village in pargana Zafarabad of tehsil Korantadih, 12 miles N.-W. of Ghazipur.	An extensive brick building excavated by Dr. Oldham now buried under earth and debris.
166	Gonda	Saheth Maheth, 12 miles from Balrampur-Akanna road in Balrampur Estate.	Ancient site .. .. ..
167	Do.	Saheth Maheth (Sravasti).	Ancient site about 150 paces from end to end near the village of Bhitti, about 2½ miles N.-W. of Maheth.
168	Do.	Do. do. ..	Mounds locally known as Penahia Jhar, Kharahua Jhar, Ora Jhar situated on the road from Balrampur near the ancient remains of Saheth Maheth (Sravasti).
169	Do.	Pachran, a small village in tehsil Gonda, 18 miles north of headquarters.	A mound 20' high apparently formed of solid brick-work in which the Prithvinath Lingam copper plate grant were found.
170	Gorakhpur ..	Matha Kuar-ka-Kot situated near Kasia, 21 miles north of tehsil Deoria.	The Buddhist remains ..
171	Do.	Anrudhva near Kasia	A mound .. ..
172	Do.	Do. do. ..	Ramabhar stupa and mound
173	Do.	Khukhundu, pargana Salimpur.	Ancient site .. ..
174	Do.	Kahaon (ancient Kakubha) a small village in pargana Salimpur of tehsil Deoria, 46 miles S.-E. of Gorakhpur.	An inscribed stone pillar .. ..
175	Do.	Do. do. ..	Two ruined temples immediately to the north of the pillar.
176	Do.	Sohnag hamlet in pargana Salimpur of tehsil Deoria, 50 miles S.-E. of Gorakhpur and 3 miles S.-W. of Salimpur.	An extensive mound situated along the ancient tank.

AGRA AND OUDH—*contd.*

♣ MONUMENTS—*contd.*

Owner or owners.	Whether in use for religious purposes.	Whether an agreement exists.	Number and date of Notification confirming protection.	Remarks.	Serial No.
5	6	7	8	9	10
Private ..	Yes ..	No ..	1669-M./1133-M., dated 27th Dec. 1920.		164
Do. ..	No ..	No ..	Do.		165
Balrampur Estate.	Yes ..	No ..	706-M.S./110-M.S.—1927, dated 27th August 1928.		166
Do. ..	Yes ..	No ..	1669-M./1133-M., dated 27th Dec. 1920.		167
Do. ..	Yes ..	No ..	Do.		168
Private ..	Yes ..	No ..	Do.		169
Government..	Yes ..		1645-M./1133, dated 22nd Dec. 1920.		170
Private ..	Yes ..	No ..	Do.		171
Do. ..	Yes ..	No ..	Do.		172
Do. ..	Yes ..	No ..	706-M.S./110-M.S.—1927, dated 27th August 1928.		173
Do. ..	Yes ..	No ..	1669-M./1133-M., dated 27th Dec. 1920.		174
Do. ..	Yes ..	No ..	Do.		175
Do. ..	Yes ..	No ..	Do.		176

Serial No.	District.		Locality.	Name of monument.
1	2		3	4
177	Gorakhpur ..	..	Chaora village, 6 miles to the north of Mithabel.	Three high conical mounds of brick which are evidently the ruins of stupas situated immediately to the north of the high road exactly opposite to Bhopa which is ¼ mile to the N.-W. of Chaora.
178	Do.	..	Rudarpur, pargana Silhat, 30 miles S.-E. of Gorakhpur.	Ancient site ..
179	Do.	..	Rudarpur town in pargana Silhat of tehsil Hata on the eastern bank of the Manjue river 27 miles S.-S.-E. of Gorakhpur.	Colossal statue of Vishnu 11' in height under a tree to the east of Rudarpur.
180	Do.	..	Do. do. ..	A high square-shaped mound close to the west of Rudarpur.
181	Do.	..	Chetiaon, a small village in pargana Sindhua Jobna of tehsil Parauna, 47 miles S.-E. of Gorakhpur.	A large Dih or mound, the north eastern corner of which is situated at a distance of less than ¼ mile to the S.-W. of the village of Fazilnagar. The mound measures 1,900' × 900'.
182	Do.	..	Do. do. ..	A circular mound about 270' in diameter, the remains of a stupa, at a distance of about 650' to the S.-W. of the great mound.
183	Do.	..	Do. do. ..	A mound 170' in circumference situated on the eastern extension of the above stupa site.
184	Do.	..	Do. do. ..	A mound of ruins called Sareya on the west bank of the Sareya Tal.
185	Do.	..	Do. do. ..	A very large mound of brick ruins called Asmanpur Dih at a distance of 3½ miles due south of Chetiaon.
186	Do.	..	Do. do. ..	A large flat-topped mound of ruins named Jharmatiya about 3½ miles to the N.-E. of Chetiaon.
187	Do.	..	Padrauna or Parauna tehsil, 49 miles N.-N.-E. of Gorakhpur.	A large mound covered with broken bricks and a few statues to the south of Padrauna. It measures 220' × 120' × 14' (high).
188	Do.	..	Amaoni, a village about 2 miles to the north of Rudarpur.	A conical stupa-shaped mound ..
189	Do.	..	Tarakulwa, a large village in pargana Shahjahanpur of tehsil Hata, 40 miles S.-S.-E. of Gorakhpur.	A very high Dih or mound, apparently the remains of a Buddhist stupa.

AGRA AND OUDH—*contd.*

MONUMENTS—*contd.*

Owner or owners.	Whether in use for religious purposes.	Whether an agreement exists.	Number and date of Notification confirming protection.	Remarks.	Serial No.
5	6	7	8	9	10
..	..		1669-M./1133-M., dated 27th Dec. 1920.		177
Private ..	No ..		706-M.S./110-M.S.—1928, dated 27th August 1928.		178
Do. ..	Yes ..	No ..	1669-M./1133-M., dated 27th Dec. 1920.		179
Do. ..	No ..	No ..	Do.		180
Do. ..	Yes ..	No ..	Do.		181
Do. ..	Yes ..	No ..	Do.		182
Do. ..	Yes ..	No ..	Do.		183
Do. ..	No ..	No ..	Do		184
Do. ..	Yes ..	No ..	Do		185
Do. ..	Yes ..	No ..	Do.		186
Do. ..	Yes ..	No ..	Do.		187
Do. ..	No ..	No ..	Do.		188
Do. ..	No ..	No ..	Do.		189

Serial No.	District.	Locality.	Name of monument.
1	2	3	4
190	Gorakhpur	Bhagalpur on the left bank of the Ghagra exactly opposite Turtipur in Tappa Balia.	Inscribed monolith standing about ½ mile east of village Bhagalpur.
191	Farrukhabad	Sankissa	Ancient remains
192	Do.	Do.	The tank of the Naga called Karewar or Kandayat Lal to the S. E. of the Sankissa ruins.
193	Do.	Kanauj	Mound known as ' Old Fort '
194	Do.	Pakhna-Bihar village in Sadar tehsil, 20 miles west of Fatehgarh close to Sankissa.	Site of an old Buddhist Vihara to the south of the village.
195	Hardoi	Bansa village, 6 miles N.-E. of Mallawan.	A large Dih covered with broken bricks and pottery and crowned with a small ruined temple of the 10th century A. D.
196	Hamirpur	Sakrra, 2 miles from Pahra situated on the bank of Barsi tank in Mahoba tehsil.	Jain temples
197	Do.	Do. do.	Brahmanical temple
198	Do.	Mahoba	Foundation of temple with five elephant statues in Madan Sagar Lake.
199	Do.	Do.	Rahilya temple
200	Do.	Do.	Kakramarh temple in Madan Sagar Lake
201	Do.	Do.	The palace of Raja Paramardideva or Parmal, situated on the top of the hill fort.
202	Do.	Do.	A small stone pillar called Alha-ki-lat 9¼' high, standing in the S.-E. quarter of the city called Dariba.
203	Do.	Do.	Twenty-four rock-hewn images of the Tirthankaras with inscriptions dated S. 1206 on a hillock on the S.-E. bank of the Madan Sagar Lake.
204	Do.	Makarbai, small village in tehsil Mahoba, 10 miles N.-E. of tehsil.	Ruins of a large granite temple situated 10 miles to the north of the village.

Owner or owners.	Whether in use for religious purposes.	Whether an agreement exists.	Number and date of Notification confirming protection.	Remarks.	Serial No.
5	6	7	8	9	10
R. N. W. Railway.	Yes ..	No ..	1645-M./1133, dated 22nd Dec. 1920.		190
Government..	No ..		2616-M./367-45, dated 27th Oct. 1915.		191
Do. ..	No ..		1669-M./1133-M., dated 27th Dec. 1920.		192
Do. ..	No ..		Do. ..	Two tombs are in use for religious worship.	193
Do. ..	No ..		Do		194
Private ..	Yes ..	No ..	Do.		195
Government Nazul.	No ..		1645-M./1133, dated 22nd Dec. 1920.		196
Do. ..	No ..		Do.		197
Do. ..	No ..		Do.		198
Do. ..	No ..		572-M./367-67. 5th April 1914.		199
Do. ..	No ..		Do.		200
Do. ..	No ..		1669-M./1133-M., dated 27th Dec. 1920		201
Government	No ..		Do.		202
Private ..	No ..	No ..	Do.		203
			Do.		

Serial No.	District.	Locality.	Name of monument.
1	2	3	4
205	Hamirpur	Makarbai, small village in tehsil Mahoba, 10 miles N.-E. of tehsil.	Makarbai temple ..
206	Do. ..	Sirisagar, village in tehsil Mahoba, 65 miles south of Hamirpur.	A fine tank called Baratal with an island bearing the ruins of a large Chandella temple.
207	Do. ..	Kabrais, town in tehsil Mahoba, 43 miles south of Hamirpur.	The Brahm Tal, an extensive tank whose embankment has the form of a segment. On this embankment is a ruined Chandella temple and in the middle of the lake the ruins of a baithak.
208	Do. ..	Urwara, tehsil Mahoba	Temple, a flat-roofed building in village ..
209	Do.	Barai Talao, about 4 miles east of Makarbai.	Middle-sized temple of which the dome has fallen, and the embankment of an almost dry tank.
210	Do. ..	Do. do. ..	A large two-roofed hall in a ruinous condition ..
211	Do. ..	Sijari ..	Sijari temple .. ..
212	Do. ..	Akona, 8 miles south of tehsil Kulpahar and 68 miles S.-W. of Hamirpur.	Four Chandella temples and a small masonry tank
213	Do. ..	Charna and Patkari villages, 6 miles to the west of Kulpahar.	Ruins of two granite temples at Charna and a large tank at Patkari.
214	Do. ..	Paraohari, about 13 miles S.-W. of Kulpahar.	An old well with an inscription of Samvat 755 .
215	Do. ..	Kulpahar	The ruins of a palace on a hill ..
216	Do.	Rawatpur, a village about 4 miles S.-E. of Kulpahar.	A large Chandella tank on the embankment of which stands a large ruined temple of the earliest Chandella type.
217	Do. ..	Do. do.	A smaller temple of which the dome has fallen, about 300 yards distant from the above.
218	Do. ..	Sumerpur, town in tehsil Hamirpur, 9 miles south of headquarters.	Mounds covered with broken bricks, etc., and three kheras near them, viz., Lakhanpur, Mirzapur and Itara.
219	Do.	Badaupur, 2 miles to the west of Hamirpur.	An inscribed image of Samvat 1368 lying under a Nim tree in the village.

AGRA AND OUDH—*contd.*

lONUMENTS—*contd.*

Owner or owners.	Whether in use for religious purposes.	Whether an agreement exists.	Number and date of Notification confirming protection.	Remarks.	Serial No.
5	6	7	8	9	10
Government Nazul.	No ..		572-M./367-67, dated 5th April 1914.		205
Private ..	No ..	Yes ..	1669-M./1133-M., dated 27th Dec. 1920.		206
Government Nazul.	No ..		Do.		207
Do. ..	No ..	..	1645-M./1133, dated 22nd Dec. 1920.		208
Do. ..	No ..	..	1669-M./1133-M., dated 27th Dec. 1920.		209
			Do.		210
Government Nazul.	No ..		572-M./367-67, dated 5th April 1914.		211
Government	No ..	..	1645-M./1133, dated 22nd Dec. 1920.		212
Private ..	No ..	No ..	1669-M./1133-M., dated 27th Dec. 1920.		213
Government	No ..	..	Do.	.	214
Private ..	Yes ..	No .	Do.		215
Government Nazul.	No ..		Do.		216
Do. ..	No ..	..	Do.		217
Private ..	Yes . ..	No ..	Do.		218
Village property	No ..	No ..	Do.		219

Serial No.	District.	Locality.	Name of monument.
1	2	3	4
242	Jhansi	Chandpur	Inscribed slab of 13th century ..
243	Do.	Do.	Inscribed slab of 1325 Samvat ..
244	Do.	Talbehat in pargana Talbehat, tehsil Lalitpur.	Fort situated to east of village on a rocky hill about 100' high.
245	Do.	Siron Khurd, tehsil Lalitpur.	Jain temple and Torana Gateway ..
246	Do.	Pali, tehsil Lalitpur ..	Temples of Nilakantha about 1½ miles S.-W. of Pali.
247	Do.	Sironi Khurd, a small village in pargana Bansi of tehsil Lalitpur, 12 miles N.-W. of headquarters.	A huge slab 5' 10" ×4' containing a Kutila inscription of 46 lines in the reign of Mahendrapaladeva. The slab is supported on buttresses inside the compound of Santi-matha's temple.
248	Do.	Lalitpur City ..	Bansa building of Firoz Shah's time .. ..
249	Do.	Ladhaura, near Dudhai village.	Temples .. .. ..
250	Do.	Dudhai village ..	Linga or Mahadeva ..
251	Do.	Do. ..	Banbaba
252	Do.	Do. ..	Varaha near tank
253	Do.	Do. ..	Bajrang
254	Do.	Do. ..	Jain temple ..
255	Do.	Do. ..	Chhatri with Varaha
256	Do.	Do. ..	Akhara ..
257	Do.	Do. ..	Rock cut Narasimha
258	Do.	Do. ..	Bania-ki-Barat ..
259	Do.	Do. ..	Larger Surang
260	Do.	Do. ..	Lesser Surang
261	Do.	Deogarh village ..	Gupta temple .. ..
262	Do.	Do. ..	Kuraiya Bir temple .. ..
263	Do.	Do. ..	Jain temple in fort .
264	Do.	Do. ..	Varaha temple in fort ..

AGRA AND OUDH—contd.

MONUMENTS—contd.

Owner or owners.	Whether in use for religious purposes.	Whether an agreement exists.	Number and date of Notification confirming protection.	Remarks.	Serial No.
5	6	7	8	9	10
Private ..	No ..	Yes ..	1106-M./367-47-II, dated 16th Oct. 1917.		242
Do. .	No ..	Yes ..	1160-M./367-47-II, dated 16th Oct. 1927.		243
Nazul ..	Yes ..		1356-M./367-V, dated 18th Nov. 1920.		244
Private ..	Yes ..	No ..	1645-M./1133, dated 22nd Dec. 1920.		245
Do. ..	Yes ..	No ..	Do.		246
Do. ..	No ..	No ..	1669-M./1133-M., dated 27th Dec. 1920.		247
M. Nazul ..	No ..		1645-M./1133, dated 22nd Dec. 1920.		248
Private ..	No ..	Yes ..	1209-M./367-47-I, dated 9th Nov. 1917.		249
Do. ..	Yes ..	Yes ..	Do		250
Do. ..	No ..	Yes ..	Do.		251
Do. ..	No ..	Yes ..	Do.		252
Do. ..	Yes ..	Yes ..	Do. .		253
Do. ..	No ..	Yes ..	Do.		254
Do. ..	No ..	Yes ..	Do.		255
Do. ..	No ..	Yes ..	Do.		256
Do. ..	No ..	Yes ..	Do.		257
Do. ..	No ..	Yes ..	Do.		258
Do. ..	No ..	Yes ..	Do.		259
Do. ..	No ..	Yes ..	Do.		260
Do. ..	No ..	Yes ..	1162-M./367-47-III, dated 1st Nov. 1917.		261
Do. ..	No ..	Yes ..	Do.		262
Government	Yes ..		Do.		263
Do. ..	No ..		1067-M./367-47-III, dated 9th/16th Oct. 1918.		264

M7DGA   79

Serial No.	District.	Locality.	Name of monument.
1	2	3	4
265	Jhansi	Deogarh Fort ..	Ghats .. ..
266	Do.	Pachwara, tehsil Mau	Chandel temple, Pachwara on the top of a small hill.
267	Do.	Kishni Khurd, small village in tehsil Mau, 19 miles S.-E. of Jhansi.	Remains of a Chandella temple of the oldest known style.
268	Do. ..	Madanpur	Temples (Bari and Chhoti Kacheries) .. ..
269	Do.	Do. ..	Temple of Mahadeva some distance north of the tank. Its porch is gone and the shrine with its pyramidal roof is out of plumb.
270	Do.	Do.	Mudiamaor, a mediaeval rearrangement of columns.
271	Do.	Do. ..	Jain group of temples in the jungles to west of the village.
272	Do.	Do. ..	Panch Marhia .. ..
273	Do.	Do.	A large temple in front of Panch Marhia whose spire was repaired in the Bundela period.
274	Do. ..	Do.	Champainor facing the east .. ..
275	Do.	Do. ..	Two small temples one of which is sacred to the mother of Mahavira.
276	Do. ..	Do. ..	Mudimor which appears to be altogether a Bundela structure.
277	Do. ..	Maha Chokri ..	Temple .. ..
278	Do. ..	Sonrai	Temple .. ..
279	Do.	Bangaous, 1 mile to the west of the village of Phatera on the banks of the Betwa.	Ruins of a large temple of the Chandella period ..
280	Do. ..	Bharauli, 3 miles S.-E. of Bhandel.	A perfect temple of the Chandella period built mostly of granite, the interior being elegantly carved with figures.
281	Do. ..	Sirwabaran, about 4 miles east of Gursarai.	Ruined temple at the end of Rai Tal on the banks of which is a roundish boulder containing two inscriptions of Samvat 1604 and 1606.
282	Do. ..	Patha-Sagauli, about 8 miles to the S.-E. of Iriebh.	The ruins of a large Chandella temple containing a well-preserved statue of Vishnu.

AGRA AND OUDH—contd.

MONUMENTS—contd.

Owner or owners.	Whether in use for religious purposes.	Whether an agreement exists.	Number and date of Notification confirming protection.	Remarks.	Serial No.
5	6	7	8	9	10
Private ..	No ..	Yes ..	1162-M./367-47-III, dated 1st Nov. 1917.		265
Do. ..	Yes ..	No ..	1645-M./1133, dated 22nd Dec. 1920.		266
Do. ..	Yes ..	No ..	1669-M./1133-M., dated 27th Dec. 1920.		267
Do. .	No ..	No	1645-M./1133, dated 22nd Dec. 1920.		268
Do. .	No .	No ..	1669-M./1133-M., dated 27th Dec. 1920.		269
Do. ..	No	No ..	Do.		270
Do. ..	No .	No ..	Do.		271
Do. ..	No .	No ..	Do.		272
Do. ..	No ..	No ..	Do.		273
Do. ..	No ..	No ..	Do.		274
Do. ..	Yes ..	No ..	Do.		275
Do. ..	No ..	No ..	Do.		276
D. B. Nazul ..	No ..	No ..	1645-M./1133, dated 22nd Dec. 1920.		277
Private ..	No ..	No ..	Do.		278
Do. ..	Yes ..	No ..	1669-M./1133-M., dated 27th Dec. 1920.		279
Do. ..		No ..	Do.		280
Do. ..	No ..	No .	Do.		281
Do. ..	Yes ..	No ..	Do.		282

Serial No.	District.	Locality.	Name of monument.
1	2	3	4
283	Jhansi	Marha, 2 miles east of Mau.	Remains of an old Chandella temple of which the sanctum is still standing.
284	Do.	Salon, small village in tehsil Jhansi, 23 miles N.-W. of headquarters.	An old Hindu temple in a fair state of preservation constructed by the Chandellas.
285	Do.	Banpur	Ganesa Khera, an ancient site with a large-headed god who possesses eighteen hands and measures 8' by 4'.
286	Do.	Do. ..	Pali khera, a deserted site just north of the large tank.
287	Do.	Do. ..	Maniktila, a large mound where there is a collection of interesting sculptures.
288	Do.	Do.	A kiosk of four Chandella columns with two Varaha statues standing on an island of the western tank.
289	Do.	Do.	Jain temple as per plates 60 and 61 in P. C. Mukerji's Report on the antiquities of Lalitpur, about a mile south of the village.
290	Do.	Do.	A dilapidated Bandela temple with a colossal statue of Tirthankara with two short inscriptions.
291	Do.	Vijapur on the south of the tank near Bar.	A beautiful temple of Mahadeva with the usual porch and shrine elaborately carved.
292	Do.	Bhadona, a small village, 4 miles west of Talbehat.	Three temples, two of Vishnu and one of Linga Mahadeva of Gandwani type.
293	Do.	Budhni, a small hamlet on the Jamini.	Temple of the Sun god whose statue is inside it
294	Do.	Chandori	A group of large Jain figures cut in the rock near Kattighati.
295	Do.	Burhi Chanderi, about 9 miles N.-W. of the modern Chanderi.	The ancient Hindu palace called Kot with gate ..
296	Do.	Do. do.	A very interesting group of Jaina temples of which some have fallen. They are situated at Burhi Chanderi.
297	Do.	Dhanganl	A sikhara-roofed temple known as Kathoyian Marhia of which the porch is gone.
298	Do.	Dhongra	A fine Sati slab showing three-headed Mahadeva at the top and fighting scenes below.
299	Do. ..	Daulatpur	The half-fallen fane of Chandi having a shrine and a porch facing S.-W.

Owner or owners.	Whether in use for religious purposes.	Whether an agreement exists.	Number and date of Notification confirming protection.	Remarks.	Serial No.
5	6	7	8	9	10
Private ..	Yes ..	No ..	1669-M./1133-M., dated 27th Dec. 1920.		283
Gwalior State		No ..	Do.		284
Private ..	Yes ..	No ..	Do.		285
Do. ..	No ..	No ..	Do.		286
Do. ..	Yes ..	No ..	Do.		287
Do. ..	Yes ..	No ..	Do.		288
Do. ..	Yes ..	No ..	Do.		289
Do. ..	Yes ..	No ..	Do.		290
Do. .	No ..	No ..	Do.		291
Do. .	Yes ..	No ..	Do.		292
Do. ..	No ..	No ..	Do.		293
Do. .		No ..	Do.		294
Do. .		No ..	Do.		295
Do. .		No ..	Do.		296
Do. ..	No .	No ..	Do.		297
Public ..	Yes ..	No ..	Do.		298
Private ..	No ..	No ..	Do.		299

Serial No. 1	District. 2	Locality. 3	Name of monument. 4
300	Jhansi	Daulatpur	A large slab of the 7 mothers with Ganesa, lying on the bed of the valley below the temple of Chandi.
301	Do.	Gurha, a small village	The northern temple consisting of a shrine and a porch and sacred to Mahadeva or Linga. An inscription of Samvat 1014 over the lintel.
302	Do.	Do. do.	Temple to the east of the village Gurha without porch dedicated to Vishnu.
303	Do.	Morkhera, a deserted town in the jungles between Saurai and Madwara.	A tall Sati slab called Gora about 15' high bearing an inscription of Samvat 1348.
304	Do.	Morkhera, a deserted town in the jungles between Saurai and Madwara.	Ruined temple facing west with a highly sculptured entrance, of which the shrine is gone. The sanctum site has a statue of Trimurti.
305	Do.	Do. do.	Another temple site close to a big pipal tree
306	Do.	Panduon, about 4 miles west of Madanpur.	An overhanging rock with some prehistoric sculpturing, bordering the Jamini valley.
307	Do.	Satgato a little to the east of Sironi Khurd.	Remains of a large Vishnu temple round a baoli on the opposite bank of the Khasar river.
308	Do.	Surahar, an old town on the high road between Lalitpur and Chanderi.	A small temple facing west with three figures of Vishnu in niches outside.
309	Lucknow	Tikaitganj	Bridge over the Bita river and the temple attached to it.
310	Meerut	Hastinapur	The mound known as Ulta Khera and the mound of Raghunathji.
311	Do.	Loni in tehsil Ghaziabad, 29 miles S.-W. of Meerut.	Remains of a fort of Prithviraj the Chauhan ruler of Delhi.
312	Do.	Meerut	Andhra Kot, a high brick fortress supposed to have been built by Mahi.
313	Do.	Mustafabad in pargana Puth of tehsil Hapur.	Raja Karna-ka-khera said to have been founded by Karna of the Mahabharata.
314	Do.	Samva in tehsil Hapur, 13 miles south of Meerut.	Two mounds (kheras) named Khorkali and Jalalpur.
315	Mirzapur	Belkhara, about 1½ miles south of Ahraura.	Inscribed pillar

AGRA AND OUDH—contd.

MONUMENTS—contd.

Owner or owners.	Whether in use for religious purposes.	Whether an agreement exists.	Number and date of Notification confirming protection.	Remarks.	Serial No.
5	6	7	8	9	10
Private	No	No	1669-M./1133-M. dated 27th Dec. 1920.		300
Private	No	No	Do.		301
Do.	No	No	Do.		302
Do.	No	No	Do.		303
Do.	No	No	Do.		304
Do.	No	No	Do.		305
Do.	Yes	No	Do.		306
Do.	Yes	No	Do.		307
Do.	Yes	No	Do.		308
Do.	Yes	Yes	749-M./367-46, dated 2nd July 1917.		309
Do.	No	No	1669-M./1133-M., dated 27th Dec. 1920.		310
Do.	No	No	Do.		311
Do.	No	No	Do.		312
Do.	No	No	Do.		313
Do.	No	No	Do.		314
Government	No		1645-M./1133, dated 22nd Dec. 1920.		315

Serial No.	District.	Locality.	Name of monument.
1	2	3	4
316	Mirzapur	Somrath, 21 miles north of Mirzapur.	An old Siva temple .. ..
317	Do.	A fort about 18 miles from Robertsganj on the top of a hill near the Kaimur range.	A pakka masonry fort (Bijaigarh) ..
318	Do.	Buhili	Cave called Khoh, containing two early Kutila inscriptions on the rock inside. The cave is situated near the dargah of Makhdum Sahib Chiragh-i-Hind.
319	Do.	Vindhyachal ..	Kantit extending for about 1½ miles from Vindhyachal on the road leading to Mirzapur on the south bank of the Ganges.
320	Do.	Chunar ..	Durga-Khoh, about half a mile to the S.-S.-W. of the Chunar railway station.
321	Do.	Bhagdewar ..	The mound known as Sangram Sahi-ki-Pahari.
322	Moradabad ..	Bherabharatpur ..	A large mound, the site of an ancient temple, where life-sized statues and dressed stones have been discovered.
323	Do.	Karawar, in Bilari pargana on the way between Bilari and Seondra.	A large mound occupying 17 bighas and 11 biswas of land.
324	Do.	Gumthal Khera, 2 miles to S.-E. of Sarthal Khera.	Gumthal Khera, an ancient mound measuring 1,600' × 1,000'.
325	Muttra ..	Muttra	Kankali Tila, Jail mound and Chaubara mound ..
326	Do. ..	Do. ..	Pali Khera mound .. ..
327	Do. ..	Do. ..	Chamunda Tila and Ahalyaganj .. ..
328	Do.	Do. ..	Sati-burj, supposed to commemorate the Sati of the widow of Raja Biharmal of Jaipur erected by her son Raja Bhagwan Das in A. D. 1570.
329	Do.	Do. ..	The portions of Katra mound which are not in the possession of Nazul tenants on which formerly stood a temple of Kesavadeva which was dismantled and the site utilised for the mosque of Aurangzeb.
330	Do.	Do. ..	Gayatri mound just outside the Bharatpur Gate of the city.

AGRA AND OUDH—*contd.*

MONUMENTS—*contd.*

Owner or owners.	Whether in use for religious purposes.	Whether an agreement exists.	Number and date of Notification confirming protection.	Remarks.	Serial No.
5	6	7	8	9	10
Maharaja of Benares.	Yes ..	No ..	1645-M./1133, dated 22nd Dec. 1920.		316
Government..	No ..	..	Do.		317
Do. ..	No ..		1669-M./1133-M., dated 27th Dec. 1920.		318
Rani of Bijaipur.	No ..	No ..	Do.		319
Private ..	Yes ..	No ..	Do.		320
Do. ..	Yes ..	No ..	1569-M./308-1923-D., dated 23rd May 1984.		321
Do. ..	Yes ..	No ..	1669-M./1133-M., dated 27th Dec. 1920.		322
Do. ..	No ..	No ..	Do.		323
Do. ..	Yes ..	No ..	Do.		324
Do. ..	Yes ..	No ..	706-M.S./110-M.S.—1927, dated 27th August 1928.		325
Do. ..	No ..	No ..	Do.		326
Do. ..	Yes ..	No ..	1570-M./367-9, dated 5th July 1923.		327
Do. .	Yes ..	No ..	1669-M./1133-M., dated 27th Dec. 1920.		28
Dr. ..	Yes ..	No ..	Do.		329
Do. ..	Yes ..	No ..	706-M.S./110-M.S.—1927, dated 27th August 1928.		330

Serial No.	District.	Locality.	Name of monument.
1	2	3	4
331	Muttra	Muttra ..	Gopal Khera situated to the north of Muttra junction railway station.
332	Do. ..	Do. ..	Girdharpur, a very large site, half a mile north of Pali Khera mound at Muttra. There are four distinct mounds on this site, three of which have been partially excavated, namely, one by Mr. Grouse, two by Rai Bahadur Pandit Radha Krishna.
333	Do. ..	Do. ..	The site of an ancient pokhar (pushkarini) about three miles from Muttra on the road to Govardhan containing 4 inscribed monolithic stairways.
334	Do. ..	Muttra District ..	Ancient sculptures, carvings, images, bas-reliefs, inscriptions, stones, and like objects, in the district of Muttra.
335	Do. ..	Mauza Ral near Bhadar, about 11 miles from Muttra.	A mound .. .. ..
336	Do.	Shahpur Ghosana, 3 miles N.-E. of Muttra.	An extensive site containing a high mound about 100' square, apparently a fort with ramparts and corner turrets.
337	Do.	Bajna village, 4 miles distant from Muttra City.	Ancient site .. ..
338	Do. ..	Kota a small village in Sadr tehsil, 3 miles north of Muttra.	A large mound to the north of the Kund which has yielded many sculptured pillars.
339	Do. ..	Kosi on Muttra and Bharatpur road, 9 miles from Muttra.	A small mound containing what appears to be a ruined brick stupa locally known as Chavar and situated about 200 yards to the west of the village.
340	Do. ..	Brindaban	Old temple of Radha Ballabh .. ..
341	Do. ..	Do. ..	Old temple of Jugal Kishore .. ..
342	Do. ..	Do. ..	Old temple of Gobind Deo ..
343	Do. ..	Mauza Sonauth near Nagla Jhenga.	A mound .. .. ..
344	Do. ..	Mat ..	Ancient site at a distance of 1 mile from Mat village and containing fragments of images.
345	Do. ..	Mora ..	Ancient site, 1 mile west of Mora village and 6 miles west of Muttra.
346	Do. ..	Ganesra ..	Two mounds situated between the Chaurasi Jain temple in the village of Ganesra. One of these mounds is known as Singer Tila.

Owner or owners.	Whether in use for religious purposes.	Whether an agreement exists.	Number and date of Notification confirming protection.	Remarks.	Serial No.
5	6	7	8	9	10
Private	No	No	1669-M./1133-M., dated 27th Dec. 1920.		331
Do.	No	No	Do.		332
Do.	No	No	Do.		333
..	..	..	706-M.S./110-M.S.—1927, dated 27th August 1928.		334
Private	Yes	No	1570-M./367-9, dated 8th July 1913.		335
Government	No	..	706-M.S./110-M.S.—1927, dated 27th August 1928.		336
Do.	Yes	..	1669-M./1133-M., dated 27th Dec. 1920.		337
Private	No	No	Do.		338
Do.	Yes	No	Do.		339
Do.	No	Yes	1232-M./341, dated 6th July 1910.		340
Do.	No	No	Do.		341
Government	Yes	..	Do.		342
Private	No	No	1570-M./367-9, dated 8th July 1913.		343
Government	No	..	706-M.S./110-M.S.—1927, dated 27th August 1928.		344
Do.	Yes	..	Do.		345
Private	No	No	Do.		346

Serial No. 1	District. 2	Locality. 3	Name of monument. 4
347	Mattra	Jaisinghpura ..	A mound measuring 100'×530', its centre being occupied by a small brick platform 19'×7'.
348	Do.	Barsana ..	A pillar with sanskrit inscription dated S. 1688 in the flanking towers of the Bhanokhar tank.
349	Do.	Mahaban	A high mound marking the old fort situated inside the town.
350	Nainital	Kota in tehsil Bhabar	The temple of Devipur on the banks of the Kosi river on a low range of wooded hills.
351	Do. ..	Dhikoli village in pargana Kota of tehsil Bhabar.	Remains of ancient buildings locally identified with Vairatapattana.
352	Sultanpur ..	Raipur, Tikri Shahgarh and Bitah near Amethi.	Extensive brick-strewn mounds, undoubtedly the ruins of Buddhist cities.
353	Do. ..	Bhagupur, village near Musafirkhana tehsil.	A group of ruined brick temples of the 10th century locally called Taligarhi.
354	Do.	Sultanpur	A large Dih called Majhargaon, 750' square, with brick towers at the four corners.

Serial No.
1

351 Mu

352 1

353

354

355

356

357

358

359

340

341

342

343

344

345

346

AGRA AND OUDH—*contd.*

MONUMENTS—*contd.*

Owner or owners.	Whether in use for religious purposes.		Whether an agreement exists.		Number and date of Notification confirming protection.	Remarks.	Serial No.
5	6		7		8	9	10
Government..	No	..			706-M.S./110-M.S.—1927, dated 27th August 1928.		347
Private ..	Yes	..	No	..	1669-M./1133-M., dated 27th Dec. 1920.		348
Government..	No	..	..		Do.		349
Private ..	Yes	..	No	..	Do.		350
Government..	No	..	..		Do.		351
Private ..	No	..	No	..	Do.		352
Do. ..	No	..	No	..	Do.		353
Do. ..	No	..	Yes	..	Do.		354

www.ingramcontent.com/pod-product-compliance
Lightning Source LLC
Chambersburg PA
CBHW021432090426
42739CB00009B/1456